THE BURIED CITY OF POMPEII

Special Edition

Text, Design, and Compilation © 1997 The Madison Press Limited
Illustrations © 1997 Greg Ruhl
Photographs © 1996 Peter Christopher (unless otherwise stated in the Picture Credits)

First published in the United States by
Hyperion Books for Children
114 Fifth Avenue
New York, N.Y. 10011-5690

First Edition
3 5 7 9 10 8 6 4 2

The artwork for each picture is prepared using gouache and acrylic.
The diagrams and maps are watercolor. This book is set in 14.5 point Berkeley book.

Library of Congress Cataloging-in-Publication Data
Tanaka, Shelley.
The buried city of Pompeii : what it was like when Vesuvius exploded / by Shelley Tanaka ;
illustrations by Greg Ruhl ; historical consultant, Elizabeth Lyding Will.
p. cm.
"A Hyperion/Madison Press Book."
Summary: Uses a fictionalized account of the life of the steward of an important estate to describe the
ancient Italian city of Pompeii and what happened to it during the eruption of Mount Vesuvius in A.D. 79.
ISBN 0-7868-1541-8
1. Italy—Antiquities—Juvenile literature. 2. Pompeii (Extinct city)—Juvenile literature.
3. Vesuvius (Italy)—Eruption, 79—Juvenile literature. 4. Excavations (Archaeology)—Italy—Pompeii (Extinct city)—Juvenile literature.
[1. Pompeii (Extinct city) 2. Vesuvius (Italy)—Eruption, 79.] I. Title.
DG70.P7T28 1997 937'.7—dc21 96-49294 CIP AC

Design and Art Direction: Gordon Sibley Design Inc.
Editorial Director: Hugh M. Brewster
Project Editor: Nan Froman
Production Director: Susan Barrable
Production Co-ordinator: Donna Chong
Color Separation: Colour Technologies
Printing and Binding: Tien Wah Press (Pte) Ltd.

The Buried City of Pompeii was produced by Madison Press Books,
which is under the direction of Albert E. Cummings.

Madison Press Books
40 Madison Avenue
Toronto, Ontario
Canada M5R 2S1

Previous page: A plaster cast of one of the volcano's victims.
Opposite page: A painting shows Pliny's uncle, who died during his attempt to
rescue people living near Vesuvius in A.D. 79.

Printed in Singapore

THE BURIED CITY OF POMPEII

What it was like when Vesuvius exploded

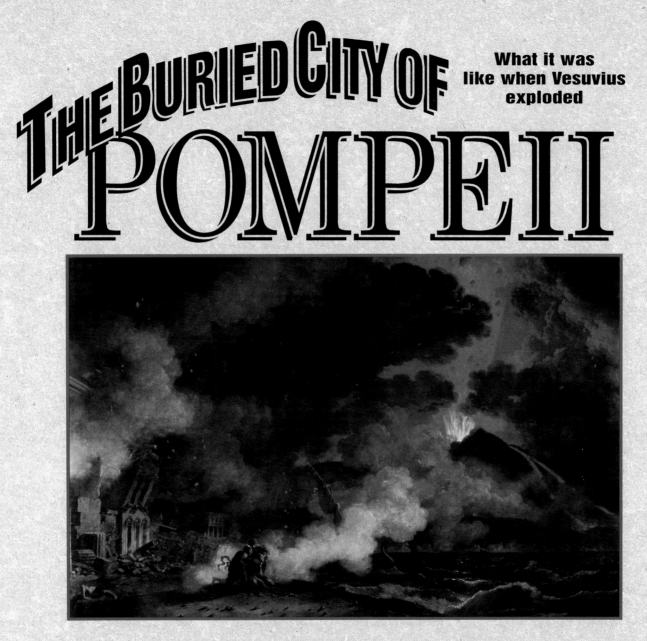

BY SHELLEY TANAKA, ILLUSTRATIONS BY GREG RUHL

Diagrams and maps by Jack McMaster, Historical consultation by Elizabeth Lyding Will
Photographs by Peter Christopher

A HYPERION/MADISON PRESS BOOK

PROLOGUE

The Bay of Naples has always been one of the most beautiful spots in Italy. The sun is hot and bright. Cool breezes blow off the blue waters of the Mediterranean Sea. The great mountain Vesuvius rises out of the countryside like a gentle giant, her slopes green with vineyards and forests.

But there is a dark side to this peaceful landscape. Far, far below the ground is an invisible battle line where two pieces of the earth's crust meet. When they bump against each other,

The victims of the volcano's wrath (above) still lie in Pompeii today below the threatening crater of Mount Vesuvius (left).

earthquakes rock the land above. And as these pieces shift, hot melted rock from deep within the earth can rise up to the surface. It builds up within the earth's crust until the great pressure forces it to escape through the mouths of volcanic mountains.

This is what happened almost two thousand years ago, when Vesuvius suddenly erupted one hot summer afternoon. As people watched in fear and horror, hot rock, gas, and ash spewed out of the mountain. By the next morning the surrounding countryside was completely buried.

Today the shoulders of Vesuvius are once again green and peaceful. But at the foot of the mountain's southern slope lies moving evidence of the tragedy that swept over the land so long ago.

The ancient Roman city of Pompeii sits there, ruined and silent. Yet there are eerie reminders of the life that once filled the city. The cobblestoned streets still show the ruts left by the wheels of Roman wagons and chariots. Fountains mark the street corners where the townspeople once gathered. A giant amphitheater, with enough seats for 20,000, stands in the corner of town. Pillars and arches still tower majestically against the sky, giving some hint of the magnificent temples to which they once belonged. Crumbling walls are all that remain of many shops, restaurants, and homes.

One such house lies near the south end of town. Known today as the House of the Menander, it was uncovered by archaeologists seventy years ago.

ITALY

Mt. Vesuvius
Pompeii

MEDITERRANEAN SEA

Right away, excavators knew that this was no ordinary home. The house took up almost a whole city block. The walls and floors were decorated with especially fine mosaics and paintings. There was an elegant private bath suite containing a dressing room, a hot steam room, and an atrium with a sunken basin for bathing. The house had a library and a huge dining room for entertaining. Even the slaves' quarters were large, and there was a spacious apartment for the head servant, the family steward.

Then, in a small cellar room below the kitchen, diggers found hidden treasure tucked away in two big wooden chests. To whom had the treasure belonged? Had the residents of the house tried to save it when volcanic gases and pumice began to smother the city? And what had happened to the people who were living in the house? Had they escaped or perished?

The answer came when archaeologists uncovered the steward's apartment. In a small room were two bodies. The skeleton of a man lay face down on a bed. And at the foot of the bed, wedged against the wall, was the skeleton of a little girl...

The House of the Menander as seen from the air (above) and in an old photograph (right) from when it was first excavated. (Left) Wheel ruts and stepping stones in the city's streets.

PART ONE

POMPEII

August 24, A.D. 79 — Morning

Eros the steward looked around in dismay. The sounds of scraping and hammering echoed through the house. Workmen heaved heavy clay containers full of plaster, piling them against one of the fluted columns. Dust lay everywhere.

Eros knelt down and inspected the low wall that surrounded the sunny garden courtyard. Would the renovations ever be finished? There was still so much to do before the master moved back into the house.

Like most of the buildings in Pompeii, the house had been badly damaged during a terrible earthquake that had rocked the city seventeen years earlier. Much of the

Today archaeologists are replanting garden courtyards such as this one, at the House of the Menander, with plants similar to those that grew in A.D. 79.

town was still being rebuilt, and it was difficult to find good workmen. Not many were skilled enough to repair the handsome wall paintings that lined the spacious reception rooms. Even fewer could restore the delicate mosaic floors of the master's fine private bath suite. For years the house had stayed empty, while the master and his family were away. But now the family had decided to return. It was Eros's job to make sure the house was ready for them.

It was a huge responsibility. He already had many important duties. He ran the master's vineyards and market gardens at the south end of the city. He kept the slaves in order. And he had a young daughter, Silvia, his only family since the death of her mother.

Still, it would be a great day when the master and mistress returned. Eros imagined them entering the atrium, the slaves strewing flowers in their path as they inspected each room of the house. It would be good to see the large dining room alive again with music, laughter, and important guests from Rome.

Soon it would be time to put the family silver on display. Eros was looking forward to opening those big wooden chests in the cellar. He would unwrap and polish each beautiful goblet himself.

A slight tremor rocked the floor. Two garden hoes that had been leaning against the wall clattered to the ground. Eros grabbed a pillar and waited, but the tremor died down as quickly as it had begun.

The builders barely paused in their work. Earth tremors were not uncommon in Pompeii, and many people took them for granted. Some young people couldn't even remember the big earthquake that had once destroyed half the city.

Eros looked closely at a split running down one of the columns. Was that a fresh crack? He couldn't remember seeing it before.

He shook his head. After all the work that had been done on the house, he couldn't bear the thought of dealing with any new repairs.

THE HOUSE OF THE MENANDER

This house is one of the largest and most luxurious in Pompeii, and it occupies almost a whole city block. Its owner was Quintus Poppaeus, a wealthy citizen who was related to a former emperor's wife. The house takes its name from a famous portrait of the ancient Greek poet Menander

(above) painted on one of the walls surrounding the garden courtyard. This plan (right) shows how the house might have looked when full of guests.

Excavation of the huge dining room revealed rooms of an even older house underneath (below).

Snack bar

Stables

Slaves' quarters

Eros's bedroom

Eros's apartment

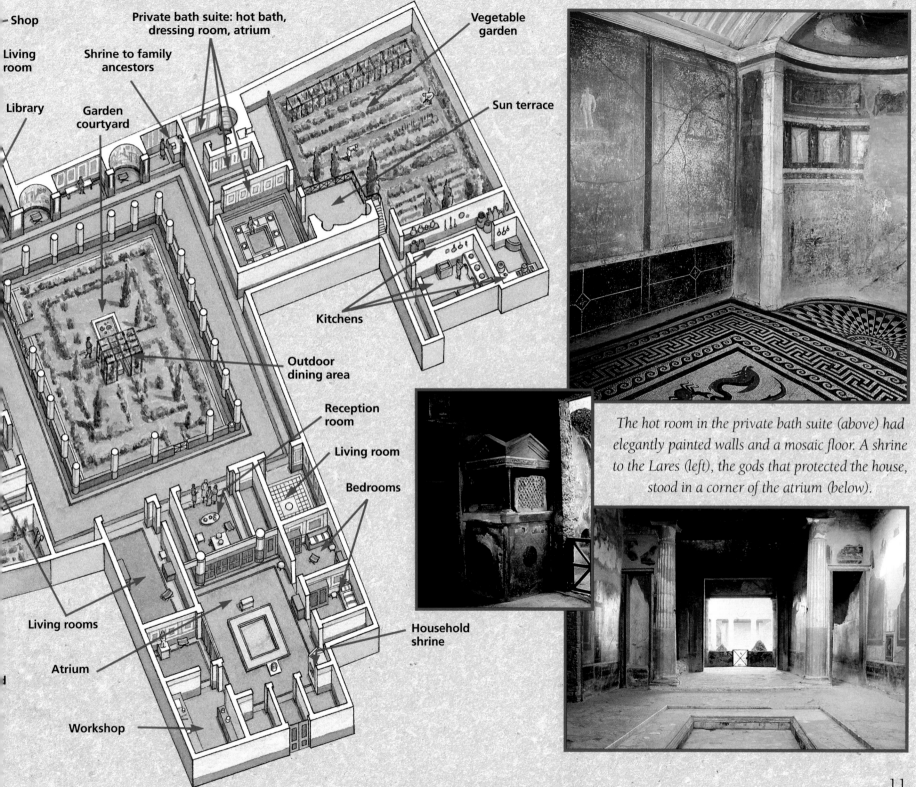

Shop

Living room

Library

Garden courtyard

Shrine to family ancestors

Private bath suite: hot bath, dressing room, atrium

Vegetable garden

Sun terrace

Kitchens

Outdoor dining area

Reception room

Living room

Bedrooms

Living rooms

Atrium

Workshop

Household shrine

The hot room in the private bath suite (above) had elegantly painted walls and a mosaic floor. A shrine to the Lares (left), the gods that protected the house, stood in a corner of the atrium (below).

11

He picked up the hoes. They'd been left by some careless slave, no doubt. He would carry them back to his apartment. He kept all the farm tools there, handing them out to the slaves every morning before they headed off to work in the vineyards. It was a good way to keep track of who was working where.

He cut across the courtyard and past the library, then walked down the narrow hall to his quarters. He had a large apartment, with its own entrance, atrium, and a small garden. From here he had a good view of the hall that ran past the slaves' sleeping cubicles, so he could keep a close eye on everything.

In his room, he hung the hoes on the wall. The sun streamed into his atrium. He wanted to make his daily trip across town before it got too hot. But first he would check on Silvia.

Eros was out of breath by the time he had looked in

Entrances to many Roman houses featured a mosaic floor that showed a fierce-looking guard dog, such as the one above.

all the usual places. It was such a big house. She was not in the kitchen where she often helped the cook. She was not in the vegetable garden. She was not even in the bath suite, where the workmen sometimes gave her tiny bits of mosaic stone to play with.

He began to get annoyed. When the master returned, the girl would have to learn that she did not have free run of the entire house.

Finally he checked the stables, and there she was, as he should have guessed. She was chatting to the donkeys and playing tug-of-war with the house watchdog.

Silvia turned and waved at him happily. Her tiny bronze ring, a gift from her father, glinted in the sunlight. He opened his mouth to call her back into the house. Then he changed his mind. She should play. After all, she had the rest of her life to work.

E ros left the cool house and stepped out onto the street. A donkey cart passed slowly by. It was going to be a very hot day.

The main street of Pompeii (above) was once lined with busy shops, bakeries, snack bars, workshops, and homes. Stone fountains (left) still mark many street corners.

He headed west, passing the theater. From behind the walls came laughter and the trill of a flute, as actors and musicians rehearsed for the afternoon's performance.

He stopped for a drink at a fountain. At his feet, a stray dog was already panting in the heat. Eros splashed water over the sides of the fountain to make a puddle, and the animal lapped it up noisily.

He wandered up to the main street. The narrow sidewalks were crowded as usual, but no one was in a hurry on such a hot day. Storekeepers slouched under their awnings, lazily keeping an eye on the goods that were displayed in front of their shops. Shiny metal discs tinkled in the open doorways, where they were hung to keep away evil spirits. The smell of the sewers under the sidewalks rose up and mingled with the scents of local businesses — roses from the perfume-makers, crushed olives from the oil presses, sour grapes from the wine shop.

THE FORUM OF POMPEII

Towering columns still stand in Pompeii's forum (right). Once the heart of the city, this grand square was badly damaged by an earthquake in A.D. 62 and then buried by the eruption of Vesuvius in A.D. 79. The mountain still looms in the distance (top right). An aerial view of the forum (top left) shows how it stretched the length of several blocks. Before it was hit by disaster, the forum included long colonnades, statues of horsemen, and a huge temple dedicated to Jupiter (below).

The main street came to an end at the forum. As Eros walked into the huge square, he could feel the heat from the smooth white paving stones burning through his sandals. Tall temples, government buildings, and markets surrounded the square. Painted columns and marble and bronze statues gleamed in the sun.

The forum looked as majestic and imposing as ever, even though it still resembled a construction site in places. The earthquake had done some of its worst damage here, and piles of rubble filled every corner.

Still, it was the pride of Pompeii. The forum was the center of government, religion, and commerce. Noisy crowds filled the square at all hours of the day and even far into the night. People came to catch up on news and meet friends. Everyone had business at the forum.

Eros crossed the square to the basilica. The courts were in session. The long hall was full of spectators who had come to listen to the trials, but the speeches seemed dull today. Most of the audience was ignoring the proceedings altogether. People were chatting with friends or busily scratching graffiti on the walls and pillars.

Eros scanned the crowd for familiar faces, but he saw no one he knew, so he left. From the Temple of Jupiter came the sounds of workmen who were busy repairing one of the grandest temples in the city.

ANCIENT GRAFFITI

Graffiti can be found all over Pompeii. In places, a line of gossip or a saying may be scratched on a wall, while elsewhere painted posters urge people to vote for a political candidate or advertise a fight between gladiators. The walls of the amphitheater feature graffiti of the gladiators themselves (below) and of the trumpet players who announced their arrival into the arena (above). The words above the falling gladiator once read: *Aurelius Iulianus mirmillo*, giving his name and identifying him as a type of heavily armed gladiator.

At the *macellum*, fishmongers and meatsellers displayed their goods as usual. The area was also crawling with people who had come to town to sell their wares. Some stood in the shade of awning-covered stalls. Others carried their goods in carts, in baskets on their heads, or on their backs. They sold everything from sandals to tools, pottery, and cakes. Dogs snuffled at every cart and cloak.

"Scaurus's finest mackerel fish sauce," called one vendor, waving a clay bottle in the air.

"Fresh figs?"

"Haircut?" The crowd pressed in from all sides.

Eros pushed his way out of the market and headed toward one of the giant archways that stood at the north end of the forum. Through it he could see the familiar outline of Vesuvius, rising up like a watchful sentry. The mountain had been good to the people of Pompeii. Her slopes were covered with vineyards and olive groves. The soil was so rich that some farmers boasted they could grow five vegetable crops a year.

Eros squinted up at the mountain. Usually flocks of sheep and goats dotted the mountainside, but he could see none today. A strange mottled haze seemed to hang over the summit. Odd, on such a clear day.

But he didn't have time to think much more about it. The sound of a gong beckoned from the next corner. The forum baths were open. Eros hurried down the street toward them.

ROMAN FISH SAUCE

Garum was a salty sauce made from fish, and it had a strong odor. The Romans enjoyed it with much of their food. In Pompeii, *garum* of the highest quality was made by a man named Umbricius Scaurus. It was expensive and was sold in small clay containers (right). A mosaic in Scaurus's house shows one of these containers inscribed with his name (below).

THE FORUM BATHS

Only the forum baths were open in August of A.D. 79. The city's other public bath was still being repaired, having been damaged in the earthquake of A.D. 62. The men's section of the forum baths contained finely decorated rooms such as the *tepidarium* or warm bath (above left), with its small terracotta statues, and the *caldarium* or hot bath (above right), with its elegant marble basin. Nearby shops provided food and wine for hungry patrons of the baths.

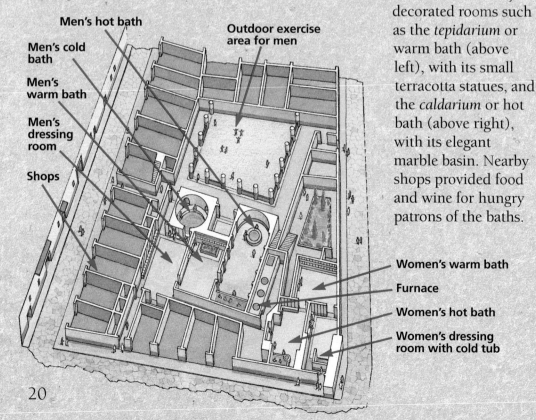

Men's hot bath

Men's cold bath

Men's warm bath

Men's dressing room

Shops

Outdoor exercise area for men

Women's warm bath

Furnace

Women's hot bath

Women's dressing room with cold tub

The baths were still quiet this early, but it wouldn't be long before the crowds came. Eros walked through the outdoor exercise area. A half dozen men were working up a sweat wrestling, running, or lifting weights. He undressed and walked through the *tepidarium*, which was warmed by a large bronze heater. Here men could lie on narrow benches while slaves massaged and cleaned their bodies with curved metal scrapers.

Beyond this was the *caldarium*, a steamy room heated by hot air that circulated under the floors and behind the walls. At one end of the room was a large bathing pool.

Eros poked the water with his foot. It was freshly heated and very hot, just the way he liked it. He eased himself into the pool. Sweat broke out on his forehead.

For many men and women, a visit to the baths was the high point of the day. It started with exercise, a massage, and a hot soak. Then came a plunge into a cold bath, followed by another massage with perfumed oils.

GLADIATORS AND THE GAMES

Many different kinds of gladiators fought in the amphitheater at Pompeii, and each had special armor and weapons. The *secutor* (left), who often fought against the net-thrower, was one of the most heavily armed. The elaborate bronze helmet (above right) was probably worn for processions into the amphitheater rather than for combat.

Gladiators learned how to fight in schools and they lived together in barracks (top right). When these barracks were excavated, fifty-two skeletons were found including some of women, children, and dogs, along with jewelry and coins.

In A.D. 59, a riot erupted in the amphitheater between spectators from Pompeii and a nearby city (right). Many were wounded and killed. After this the senate in Rome banned the games at Pompeii for ten years.

But the baths were about much more than getting clean. Customers gossiped and strolled, read and napped. In the winter, some came just to get warm. By the time the bathers emerged onto the street, relaxed, flushed, and sweet smelling, several hours had often passed.

Eros closed his eyes and listened to the conversations floating through the room. One man was complaining about a local innkeeper who put too much water in the wine he served. Another boasted about the dinner party he had attended the night before. The roasted peacock with melons, vinegar, and mustard had been magnificent. On one of the stone benches, two men were arguing over a game of dice. By the wall, a big-bellied man waved his arms dramatically as he described one of the fights that had taken place in the amphitheater that morning.

"...at first I was sure the gladiator would win. He was in full armor, with a sword as long as my leg and as sharp as a tiger's claws. His opponent? The net-thrower, armed with only a fishing net, a trident, and a dagger. But the fisherman was fast. In the blink of an eye he had the gladiator caught in his net and pinned to the ground. He held his dagger to the man's throat. The gladiator begged for mercy. The fisherman looked up at the crowd..."

Eros opened his eyes. All other conversations in the room had stopped. Everyone was listening.

Pompeii's huge amphitheater was built in 80 B.C. and is believed to be the oldest one in the world. The lower rows had the best view of the arena and were reserved for important citizens.

The storyteller's eyes gleamed. "And then...the crowd stood as one and booed. The director of the games raised his arm. He pointed his thumb to the ground and, well, it was over in seconds. There'll be one more empty bed in the gladiators' barracks tonight."

The crowd in the bath nodded in approval. The man scratched his stomach and grinned.

"The net-thrower takes on a wild bear this afternoon. My money is on the bear. By the time the day is over, the sand in the arena will be red with blood."

Eros shook his head. The amphitheater games were not to his taste. He got little pleasure from watching men and half-starved animals tear each other to pieces. And the master had once told him that the spectacles in Pompeii were tame compared with the games held in Rome. When the emperor was in attendance, the crowd could watch fights between strange and wonderful animals that they had never seen before — rhinoceroses, elephants, tigers. In one day, it was said, more than 5,000 animals had been slaughtered. In one contest, 350 gladiators had fought to the death.

Eros preferred quieter entertainments — a play at the theater, or perhaps a poetry reading or concert at the smaller *odeum*. His master loved the theater, and over the years Eros had accompanied him to many performances.

Working for such a man had given him a taste for fine things.

The men in the baths returned to their quiet conversations. Eros listened carefully. The master liked to use his private baths at home, but he would still send his steward to the public baths to pick up any useful gossip.

Eros leaned his head back against the edge of the pool. Fragrant steam filled his nostrils. Outside the walls lay the noisy, dusty street, but in here everything was dark and peaceful.

He sighed with contentment. He was a freedman working for one of the richest and most respected families in Pompeii. He had money of his own, a healthy and beautiful daughter. After his bath, he would stop at his favorite bakery and buy some fresh bread for lunch, and perhaps a sweet cake for Silvia. He would go back to the house and lay out a fine spread in the large dining room, with its view of the fountain and courtyard. He would lie back and eat a leisurely lunch. Maybe he would have a nap.

There would not always be time for such luxury. When the master returned he would need his steward for important business errands. But for now, Eros had all the time in the world.

THE THEATERS OF POMPEII

Humorous plays and pantomimes were staged at the large open-air theater (above), which seated five thousand people. On hot days, awnings could be pulled over the audience using a system of ropes and pulleys. There were even fountains to provide a cool spray during intermissions. Details from wall paintings found in Pompeii show actors during a performance (left) and a dramatic mask (middle). There was a smaller indoor theater for concerts, where instruments such as the harp and *cithara* (far right) were played.

PART TWO

POMPEII

August 24, A.D. 79 — 1 P.M.

Eros was jostled out of his doze as new bathers climbed into the hot pool. Outside, a noisy line was forming. He thought he could hear faint laughter coming from the women's baths on the other side of the wall.

He climbed out of the pool and walked over to the fountain of cold water that sat in an alcove at the end of the room. He splashed water on his face and leaned his hands on the edge of the basin. He looked down at the water through half-closed eyes. The light that streamed through the window above made the marble bottom gleam and sparkle.

He opened his eyes wider. The water in the basin had begun to

The gleaming marble basin still stands in the caldarium of the forum baths.

tremble, as if it were beginning to boil. Then a boom, like a muffled clap of thunder, seemed to come from the floor beneath him. The water sloshed over the sides of the basin, splashing at his feet.

Eros turned around. All the men in the room had stopped talking. Some grabbed for the walls and each other as the floor continued to shudder.

Surely not another earthquake, he thought, his heart sinking. He remembered all the careful restoration work that had been done at the house. Everything was so close to being finished. It would be a terrible nuisance if more damage were done now.

He clutched the sides of the basin, waiting for the tremor to stop. But it didn't. Bottles of oil crashed to the floor

in the next room. A man standing beside him was thrown off his feet. Then the window in the overhead dome began to grow dark, and soon the entire room was plunged into blackness.

Men screamed as they pushed toward the exits. A few slaves grabbed oil lamps and tried to light them with shaking hands. Finally they dropped the lamps in panic and ran.

Eros stumbled to the nearest door. Wet, naked men streamed into the street. The sky was very dark, and there was an odd yellowish cast to the air. People poured out of the surrounding buildings, their faces filled with confusion.

A pot of flowers fell from a second-story windowsill and smashed on the sidewalk below. Eros looked up. His gaze was drawn to the north, toward Vesuvius. And what he saw filled his throat with fear.

This was no earthquake.

The familiar outline of the mountain was transformed. An enormous black cloud billowed from the summit, which glowed a fiery red.

Tiny white pellets of pumice began to fall like a soft hailstorm. Eros felt as if he were being nipped by hordes of flying insects. Pieces the size of rice stuck to his hair and wet body. Bigger stones, like acorns, rolled underfoot.

People pulled their tunics over their heads and took shelter in doorways. The clatter of pumice on the cobblestones and tiled roofs grew louder, echoing through the narrow streets. It drowned out the shouts of shopkeepers who were trying to pull their wares indoors. It muffled the sharp cries of children calling for their parents.

Silvia. She was back at the house. He must get to her.

He made his way down the road, but the streets were clogged with carts and people. Everyone seemed to be heading toward the city gates. Toward the sea. Away from the mountain.

Eros tried to push his way through the crowds, but it was no use. The streets were too narrow. He turned around and headed back to the forum.

In the grand square, people fled from every building. Shoppers and merchants swarmed out of the market. Peddlers pulled their carts behind them, their goods spilling out as they ran. A bronze statue tumbled off its pedestal. From inside the Temple of Jupiter came a long scream. The cry was suddenly cut short by a thundering crash within the building.

Eros pushed his way through the throng. When he got to the bottom of the forum, he stopped in dismay. Pompeii's main street, as far as he could see, was filled with people, and they all seemed to be coming his way. He closed his eyes and began to shove past them.

The house was halfway across town. How long would it take him to get there?

Donkeys, carts, dogs, and people were everywhere. Benches in front of the shops had been overturned. Looters grabbed jugs and food. A fighter from the amphitheater, the net-thrower, thundered past. He still wore his shoulder armor, and he waved his dagger wildly to clear a path in front of him.

The pumice fell steadily. Soon everything was covered with a ghostly cloak. Eros stumbled over one of the stepping stones in the middle of the road. His bare feet were bloody.

In front of him, a rich man in a sedan chair was cursing at the four slaves who were trying to carry his litter down the street. Their way was blocked by a cart that had been abandoned and overturned. The slaves were clumsily trying to make their way over it, while their master stayed in his chair and screamed at them.

"You fool!" someone yelled. "Why don't you just get out and walk? You're blocking the way for others!" As Eros watched, one of the slaves finally dropped his corner of the litter and fled. The rich man tumbled out onto the street and was trampled by the crowd.

By the time Eros reached his own block, he was limping. He hurried into the house. It was very quiet. In the garden, the workmen had disappeared.

He ran down the hallway, calling for Silvia. There was no answer. He headed for the stables.

FROM SLAVE TO FREEDMAN

Pompeii was home to a large number of slaves, who often did the same work as free people. They might be craftsmen or shopkeepers; they could be doctors or teachers, even gladiators or farmers. A slave was considered a member of his or her master's family, and any Roman citizen could give freedom to a loyal slave. A child born to a slave who had obtained his freedom was equal to any Roman citizen. In the stone relief (above) slaves carry an empty sedan chair.

She was on her knees, trying to free the dog from his rope. The animal was thrashing in panic. Eros could see that her face and arms were already scratched. He scooped her up and ran back into the house. He tried not to listen to the frenzied howls behind him, as the dog strained at its rope.

In the courtyard, a stew of fallen pumice floated in the fishpond. The pumice was coming down thickly now. It filled the courtyard like snow.

Eros stopped, panting. The house trembled and shook. It was crumbling before his eyes. His master would never have a chance to see the repairs now, to thank his loyal steward for all his effort.

Eros brushed a piece of pumice from Silvia's tear-stained cheek. Grains of it, like gravel, were tangled in her hair. She began to cough and pressed her face into her father's neck.

He ran down the narrow sloping corridor to his quarters. He put Silvia down on the bed. Then he went to the door and looked out. Across the street, a balcony crashed to the ground.

When Eros looked north now he could no longer see the mountain. It was as if a thick black blanket were gradually being lowered over the face of the city. The air was filled with a sharp, deadly smell.

Eros closed the door and went back inside. He looked down the hall past the slaves' quarters. From around the corner he could hear voices calling, the sound of running footsteps. He began to walk down the hall when rubble fell from the second story, blocking his way. The voices stopped.

Eros watched the dust settle around him. The passage to the rest of the house was blocked.

He tried to think clearly. Should they stay in the house and hope that the terrible storm would pass? Or should they take their chances at escape?

His ankle throbbed painfully. He would not get far carrying Silvia through the deadly downpour in the streets. Besides, how could he leave the house unattended? What about the treasure in the cellar? The master had entrusted it to his safekeeping...

He turned slowly back to his apartment. Silvia was sitting on a bucket beside the bed, her head buried in her arms. She was weeping softly.

Eros found his seal and the leather purse that contained his life's savings. He went into the bedroom and sat on the bed beside his daughter. He drew Silvia to him and held her tightly. Then he stared into his tiny courtyard and watched it slowly disappear beneath a sea of gray hail.

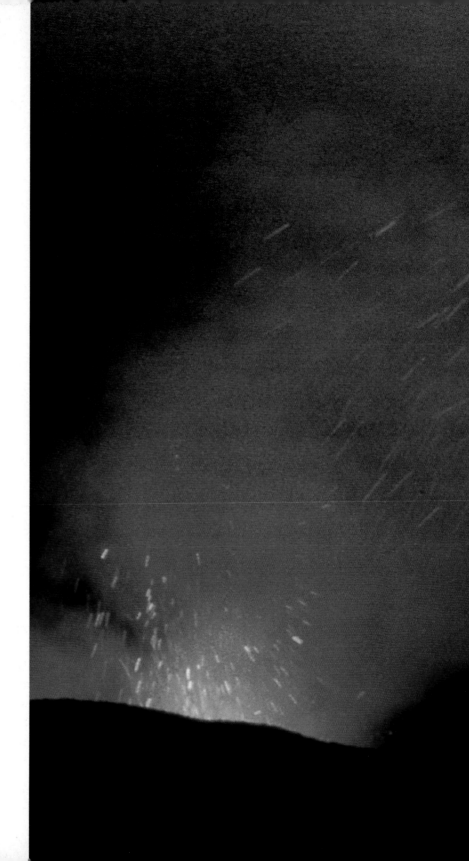

EPILOGUE

Vesuvius erupted on August 24, A.D. 79. Pompeii had been experiencing earth tremors for a few days, and many people still remembered an earthquake that had damaged much of the city seventeen years before. But they did not realize that they were living in the lap of a deadly volcano.

At about 1 P.M., the mountain roared, and her summit cracked open. A huge column of pumice and ash shot up into the air like a rocket. When the column reached the height of 12 miles (20 kilometers), it spread out like a fountain. Ash and pumice began to fall to the ground.

In horror, the people of Pompeii had to decide whether to flee or stay. Most chose to run, and soon the gates were clogged with humans and pack animals trying to push their way out of the city. Others hid in their homes, hoping that by some miracle, the rain of fire would soon stop.

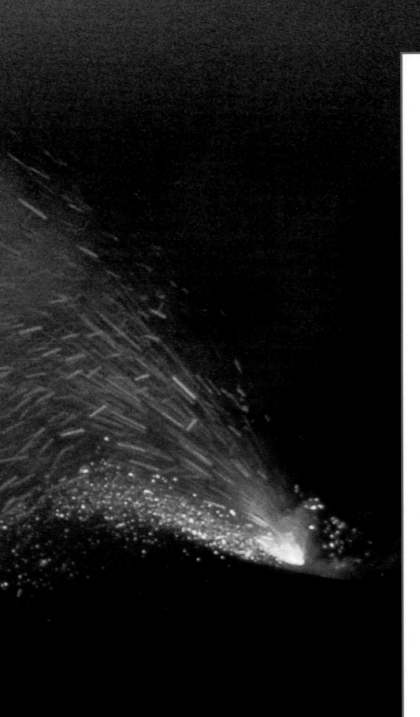

THE DAY VESUVIUS EXPLODED

On August 24, A.D. 79, a mushroom-shaped cloud of pumice and ash rose from the mouth of Vesuvius (top right). Soon pumice began to fall steadily on Pompeii, followed later by a rain of fine ash. The town of Herculaneum, upwind from the volcano, received a lighter dusting of ash. Early the next morning, surges of hot ash and gas began to race down the mountain, followed by a flow of hot ash, rock, and pumice. Herculaneum was hit first; Pompeii was buried several hours later (bottom right). Stromboli, an island volcano in the Mediterranean, shows "fountaining" activity (left), a bubbling of lava that is much less violent than the eruption that buried Pompeii.

Herculaneum **Pompeii**

Surge

Flow

HOW WAS POMPEII BURIED?

Scientists have examined the layers of debris that fell on Pompeii to help them understand exactly what happened when Vesuvius erupted. The first phase of the eruption consisted of a slow accumulation of pumice. Most people escaped from the city during this time. Those who remained lost their lives when the first surge of hot ash and gas sped down the mountainside. This surge left behind a deposit of hardened volcanic sand (right). While Pompeii was buried under about twelve feet (4 meters) of pumice and ash, the town of Herculaneum was overwhelmed by 65 feet (20 meters) of debris.

Ashy top soil

Fragments of lava

Ash

Fragments of lava

Sandy ash with pieces of carbonized wood

Fragments of lava

Hardened volcanic sand

Pumice

Lava pebbles

But it didn't. With every passing hour, another 6 inches (15 centimeters) of pumice covered Pompeii. By late afternoon, the sky was almost black. Roofs caved in. Walls collapsed as earth tremors rocked the city.

At midnight, the column of ash and pumice finally collapsed back to earth. That's when superhot rock and gas spewed up out of the volcano and began to flow down the mountain, smothering and burning up the countryside.

The avalanche reached the walls of Pompeii at 5:30 the next morning. The people who remained in the city died from the extreme heat, or they were suffocated as they breathed in the hot ash. Within three hours, the city was completely buried.

After the eruption, many people returned to their homes, but Pompeii lay under a sea of pumice and ash. Some got shovels and tried to uncover the bodies of their loved ones. Some searched for their strongboxes and money. Others dug down to the majestic temples and public buildings, hoping to find valuable statues or building materials. Several of these diggers were buried when the ground caved in on top of them.

Eventually, though, the survivors drifted away. And after many years, the slopes of Vesuvius were again covered with green forests and meadows.

But centuries later, people still remembered stories about an ancient buried city. And in 1748, they began to dig down to the city in earnest. At first the work was sloppy and disorganized. Treasure hunters ripped out priceless statues and artwork. Coins and vases were carted away.

HOW DO WE KNOW ABOUT THE ERUPTION OF VESUVIUS?

Much of what we know about the eruption in A.D. 79 comes from two letters written by the Roman statesman and writer, Pliny. As a teenaged boy, Pliny watched the volcano from the home of his uncle, at Misenum, across the Bay of Naples. Years later, he described what he saw in letters that have become famous as the oldest eyewitness account of a major natural disaster. Pliny's uncle sailed across the bay to rescue survivors, but raining pumice prevented him from landing near Vesuvius. He died the next day on the beach at Stabiae (right), probably overcome by the heat from the blast.

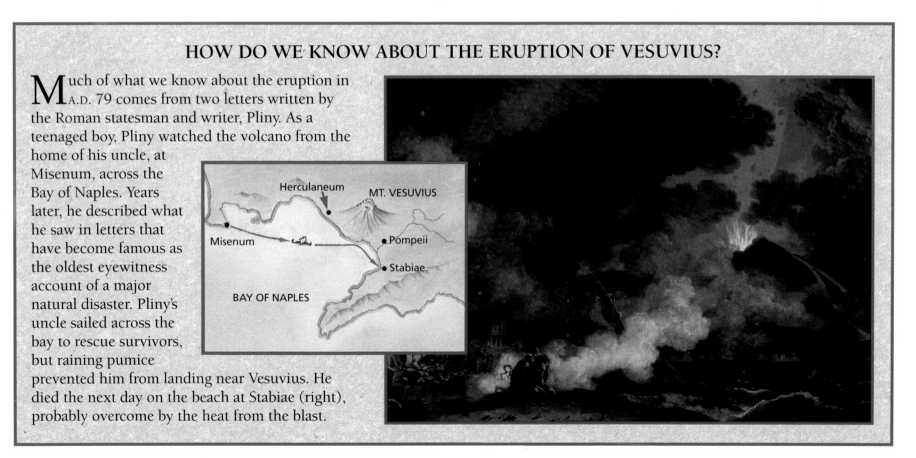

Herculaneum

MT. VESUVIUS

Misenum

Pompeii

Stabiae

BAY OF NAPLES

For 1,500 years, Pompeii had been buried under a thick blanket of pumice and ash. This material had protected the city beautifully from the air and rain. But as soon as the buildings were uncovered, they began to crumble. The brilliant paintings on the walls began to fade.

In 1860, Giuseppe Fiorelli was put in charge of the excavation. Fiorelli was an archaeologist, and he knew that the town should be uncovered in an organized and scientific way. He made detailed maps and carefully recorded each new find. He began to restore the buildings and art, instead of hauling away the most valuable pieces and leaving the rest to rot.

Over the years, the excavations continued, making Pompeii one of the oldest and most studied archaeological sites in the world. Then, between 1927 and 1932, an archaeologist named Amedeo Maiuri discovered one of the finest houses in the city, the House of the Menander. Here diggers found the remains of a grand residence that was undergoing major renovations. *Amphoras* full of plaster were found in the courtyard. Farm implements hung on the wall of the steward's apartment. In the cellar were two chests full of gold and silver coins, jewelry, and 118 beautiful silver dishes.

DISCOVERING A VILLA

Just outside Pompeii's walls lay an elegant villa, now known as the Villa of Diomedes (right). It had a beautiful garden, with an open-air dining room and a shimmering fishpond. In 1772, excavators discovered twenty skeletons in an underground terrace. Two skeletons were found near the back gate, one clutching a key, the other a bag of coins. These may have once been the master and his steward. In the late 1800s photographs were taken of the villa's ruins (above) and of excavations in Pompeii (facing page).

The diggers also found bodies. The skeleton of a dog lay in a corner of the stable yard. Several bodies were found in the hallway outside the slaves' quarters. And in the corner of a small room in the steward's apartment, a man lay on a narrow bed. He had a leather purse full of money and a seal that identified him as Eros, steward of one of the most important families in Pompeii. Nearby was the skeleton of a young girl. On the ground beside her were pieces of a tiny bronze ring engraved with a picture of a winged horse.

The two stamps of this bronze seal identify the owner as Eros of the family of Quintus Poppaeus. The seal could be carried on the finger, like a ring, or worn on a chain around the neck.

Did the skeletons in the hallway belong to servants or workmen who were in the house when the eruption occurred? Was the little girl the daughter of the steward? Had they stayed in the house to protect the treasure? Or had they for some reason been unable to run? No one knows for sure.

The skeletons cannot tell us their story. But Pompeii can still teach us a great deal about what life was like almost two thousand years ago. Every object, every building gives us a glimpse into this long-ago world.

TREASURES IN THE HOUSE OF THE MENANDER

Excavations at the House of the Menander revealed priceless treasures. Whether the skeletons now on display in this living room (right) belonged to servants in the house or workers attempting to recover belongings after the eruption remains a mystery. The same is true of a large hole in the wall of one of the smaller rooms (below). Was it the work of early excavators or hopeful thieves?

Today the House of the Menander is most famous for the hundred or more beautifully made silver pieces found in wooden chests in the cellar. Perhaps dinner guests once drank from these silver cups (above left and right). Archaeologists also found an elegant silver mirror (left) and a gold bulla (shown right at twice actual size), which would have been placed around the neck of a baby boy as a sign that he was free and not a slave.

41

THE VICTIMS OF VESUVIUS

Although most Pompeians managed to escape from the eruption, about two thousand people (one-tenth of the population) died in the city (top right). When archaeologist Giuseppe Fiorelli began excavations in 1860, he noticed shapes that looked like bodies in the hardened debris. Over the years the victims' flesh had disintegrated, leaving bones and hollow impressions in the volcanic rock. Fiorelli filled these cavities with plaster (middle right) and then chipped away the rock after the plaster had hardened (bottom right). The plaster casts show the people of Pompeii at the moment of death (facing page, left, and bottom).

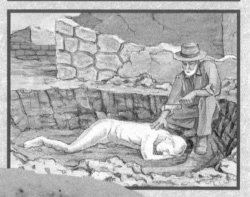

In one of the temples, the bones of an animal that had just been sacrificed were lying on the altar. In another room lay the remains of the priests' lunch — fruit, eggs, and nuts. In the forum baths, perfume bottles, bath scrapers, and more than one thousand oil lamps were found. Many buildings were covered with advertisements and messages that people had scrawled on the walls. Jugs held the remains of *garum*, the smell of the fish sauce still strong after hundreds of years. Fish, fruit, and grain were found in the market.

Pompeii shows us that the ancient Romans were very much like us in many ways. Yet they were also very different. They lived in airy, high-ceilinged houses but had little furniture. They surrounded themselves

Archaeologists found petrified 2,000-year-old eggs (bottom left) in the Temple of Isis (above). A wall painting from Pompeii suggests how the priests' lunch table in the temple might have looked (top left).

with objects that brought good luck or protected them from evil. They adored their gardens, their children, and the theater. But

they also kept slaves and loved to watch incredibly cruel sports. They spent long, lazy hours at the baths, and the wealthy ate meals so rich that vomiting was sometimes considered a normal part of a dinner party.

Thanks to Vesuvius, we can open up Pompeii like a time capsule and come face to face with an ancient civilization and its people. Yet some aspects of those people will always remain a mystery.

Wealthy Romans enjoyed fine dining (above) and would have used silver dishes such as these from the House of the Menander (left). A wall painting shows a young couple from Pompeii (above left).

It is this combination of understanding and mystery that draws more than two million people to Pompeii each year. Visitors can walk through the empty forum and imagine all of the grand columns and statues that once towered over the square. You can wander down the once-busy streets, see the stepping stones and wheel ruts in the road, poke your head into shops and homes. And you can sit in the great amphitheater and almost hear the shouts of the crowds as they cheered on the gladiators.

Meanwhile, Vesuvius still looms to the north. Since Pompeii was buried, the mountain has erupted eighty times. The last eruption was in 1944.

Never has the volcano remained quiet for so long.

POMPEII TODAY

Today the excavating and restoring of buildings in Pompeii continues (above and right). Some of the roofs and balconies of ancient villas have been rebuilt. Statues have been put back in their original spots. Gardens have been replanted with the same trees and flowers that once filled them.

Now computers are being used to catalogue finds, record excavations, and make detailed maps of the city, so that scholars all over the world can find information quickly. Restorers can create 3-D models to see how buildings might look when they are rebuilt. And with new interactive video programs, people can wander through the House of the Menander, exploring its rooms and reading about the treasures found there.

GLOSSARY

amphitheater: An oval or circular building, similar to a stadium, used for games or performances.

amphora: A large clay container with two handles and either a pointed or flat bottom that the Romans used to transport goods such as oil, wine, fruit, nuts, fish sauce, and olives.

archaeologist: A person who studies people from the past and their cultures.

arena: The central open space of an amphitheater. This word comes from the Latin word for the sand that often covered the arena floor.

atrium: The main room in a Roman house. The atrium usually contained a large basin in the floor, called an *impluvium*, to catch rainwater.

basilica: A public hall, often near the forum, used for legal trials and business.

caldarium: The room for taking a hot bath in a Roman public bath.

colonnade: A row of columns that is joined at the top.

excavator: A person who "excavates" or uncovers an object, a skeleton, or even an entire city, such as Pompeii, by digging.

freedman: A man who is no longer a slave, having been given or having bought his freedom from a master.

frigidarium: The room for taking a cold bath in a Roman public bath.

Jupiter: The king of the Roman gods.

macellum: The marketplace.

mosaic: A design or picture made by joining together small pieces of stone or glass.

odeum: The name for a small indoor theater in ancient Rome and Greece, where concerts were held.

petrified: Turned into stone.

pumice: Light volcanic rock with small holes in it, like a hard sponge.

steward: A person who manages a large house or estate belonging to someone else.

tepidarium: The warm room in a Roman public bath.

terracotta: Fine pottery of a brownish-red color, usually unglazed.

trident: A spear with three prongs used by the gladiator known as the *retiarius* or net-thrower.

PICTURE CREDITS

All photographs are by Peter Christopher and all illustrations are by Greg Ruhl unless otherwise stated. Every effort has been made to attribute correctly all material reproduced in this book. If any errors have unwittingly occurred, we will be happy to correct them in future editions.

Front cover: (Bottom right) Scala/Art Resource, NY

Back cover: (Top right) Erich Lessing/Art Resource, NY (Bottom right) Mary Evans Picture Library

Front flap: Courtesy of Robert I. Curtis

3: Painting by Pierre-Henri de Valenciennes, the Musée des Augustins, Toulouse, France

5: Grape vine motif throughout by Jack McMaster. Leonard von Matt/Photo Researchers, Inc.

6: (Map) Jack McMaster

8: Courtesy of Elizabeth Lyding Will

10: (Top) Scala/Art Resource, NY (Bottom) Courtesy of Elizabeth Lyding Will

10-11: (Diagram) Jack McMaster

11: (Top) Leonard von Matt/Photo Researchers, Inc. (Middle) Courtesy of Robert I. Curtis (Bottom) Scala/Art Resource, NY

16: (Diagram) Jack McMaster

16-17: (Middle) Erich Lessing/Art Resource, NY

17: Graffiti redrawn by Jack McMaster

19: (Left and right) Courtesy of Robert I. Curtis

20: (Top left and right) Erich Lessing/Art Resource, NY (Bottom) Diagram by Jack McMaster

22: (Diagram) Jack McMaster (Top middle) Scala/Art Resource, NY (Bottom) Erich Lessing/Art Resource, NY

25: (Left and bottom left and right) Erich Lessing/Art Resource, NY

26: Erich Lessing/Art Resource, NY

34-35: Jonathan Blair/National Geographic Image Collection

35: (Diagrams) Jack McMaster

36: (Diagram) Jack McMaster

37: Painting by Pierre-Henri de Valenciennes, the Musée des Augustins, Toulouse, France (Inset map) Jack McMaster

38: (Top) Mary Evans Picture Library (Diagram) Jack McMaster

39: Mary Evans Picture Library

40: (Diagram) Jack McMaster (Bottom) Courtesy of Elizabeth Lyding Will

40-41: (Middle) Courtesy of Elizabeth Lyding Will

41: (Top left and right, bottom left and right) Courtesy of Anna Marguerite McCann

42: Alinari/Art Resource, NY

43: (Top) Erich Lessing/Art Resource, NY (Bottom) Mary Evans Picture Library (Diagrams) Jack McMaster

44: (Top and bottom left) Courtesy of Hugh Brewster (Right) Erich Lessing/Art Resource, NY

45: (Left) C.M. Dixon (Right) Erich Lessing/Art Resource, NY (Bottom) Alinari/Art Resource, NY

46: David Hiser/Photographers Aspen

RECOMMENDED FURTHER READING

The Secrets of Vesuvius
by Sara C. Bisel
(Scholastic, Inc.)

The fascinating story of Sara Bisel's excavation of skeletons discovered at Herculaneum, including a re-creation of life in the ancient town in A.D. 79.

Pompeii
by Peter Connolly
(Oxford University Press)

A detailed, fully illustrated account of what it was like to live in Pompeii in A.D. 79.

How Would You Survive As an Ancient Roman?
by Anita Ganeri
(Franklin Watts)

Words and pictures show how you would live as an ancient Roman, whether you were a citizen, a soldier, or a slave, from what you did each day to what you wore and ate.

Ancient Rome
by Simon James
(Dorling Kindersley Publishing Inc., U.S.; Stoddart Publishing Co. Limited, Canada)

Hundreds of photographs and illustrations bring the civilization of ancient Rome to life, from its emperors to its slaves.

Ancient Rome
by Simon James
(Hamlyn Children's Books/Reed International Books Ltd.)

All about life during the Roman Empire, including four see-through pages which look inside a Pompeii town house, the public baths, a theater, and an auxiliary fort.

Volcano and Earthquake
by Susanna van Rose
(Dorling Kindersley Publishing Inc., U.S.; Stoddart Publishing Co. Limited, Canada)

Describes the power of volcanoes and earthquakes, volcanoes on other planets, what it is like to be a volcanologist, and more.

ACKNOWLEDGMENTS

Madison Press Books would like to thank the following individuals for their invaluable assistance: Our principal consultant, Elizabeth Lyding Will, Professor Emeritus of Classics at the University of Massachusetts at Amherst; Peter S. Allen; Antonio Barbato; Steven Carey of the University of Rhode Island Graduate School of Oceanography; Robert I. Curtis of the University of Georgia; Harrison T. Eiteljorg, II; Joseph Gisini; Norma Goldman of Wayne State University; Ann O. Koloski-Ostrow; Carole Lazio; Anna Marguerite McCann of Boston University; Alison Reid; and Madeleine White of Multilingua International Ltd.